W9-BYB-271

# The Silence Now

## New and Uncollected Earlier Poems

## Books by May Sarton

# The Silence Now

## New and Uncollected Earlier Poems

### By MAY SARTON

**W·W·NORTON & COMPANY**

*New York · London*

Copyright © 1988 by May Sarton
All rights reserved.
Published simultaneously in Canada by Penguin Books Canada Ltd., 2801 John
Street, Markam Ontario L3R 1B4. Printed in the United States of America.

The text of this book is composed in Janson Alternate, with display type set in
Deepdene Italic. Compostion and manufacturing by The Haddon Craftsmen, Inc.


First Edition


Library of Congress Cataloging-in-Publication Data
Sarton, May. 1912–
        The silence now: new and uncollected earlier poems/by May
Sarton.—1st ed.
        p. cm.
    I. Title.
    PS3537.A832S54    1988
811'.52—dc19                                                                 88–12429

ISBN 0-393-02651-5

W. W. Norton & Company, Inc., 500 Fifth Avenue, New York, N. Y. 10110
W. W. Norton & Company Ltd., 37 Great Russell Street, London WC1B 3NU

1 2 3 4 5 6 7 8 9 0

# Contents

# III Earlier Poems

# IV

Some of these poems first appeared in
*Bay Windows, Calyx, Cream City
Review, Francis Marion Review, The
Kentucky Poetry Review, New York
Quarterly, Poetry, Puckerbrush Review,
Transatlantic Review, Yale Literary
Magazine, Women in the Arts,* and in
*The Phoenix Again,* published by
William B. Ewart in a limited edition.

# Author's Note

Most of these poems have been
written in the last few years, except
for the poems in Part III, written
much earlier, but never before placed
in a collection.

# Part I

# New Year Resolve

The time has come
To stop allowing the clutter
To clutter my mind
Like dirty snow,
Shove it off and find
Clear time, clear water.

Time for a change,
Let silence in like a cat
Who has sat at my door
Neither wild nor strange
Hoping for food from my store
And shivering on the mat.

Let silence in.
She will rarely speak or mew,
She will sleep on my bed
And all I have ever been
Either false or true
Will live again in my head.

For it is now or not
As old age silts the stream,
To shove away the clutter,
To untie every knot,
To take the time to dream,
To come back to still water.

# The Silence Now

These days the silence is immense.
It is there deep down, not to be escaped.
The twittering flight of goldfinches,
The three crows cawing in the distance
Only brush the surface of this silence
Full of mourning, the long drawn-out
Tug and sigh of waters never still—
The ocean out there, and the inner ocean.

Only animals comfort because they live
In the present and cannot drag us down
Into those caverns of memory full of loss.
They pay no attention to the thunder
Of distant waves. My dog's eager eyes
Watch me as I sit by the window, thinking.

At the bottom of the silence what lies in wait?
Is it love? Is it death? Too early or too late?
What is it I can have that I still want?

My swift response is to what cannot stay,
The dying daffodils, peonies on the way.
Iris just opening, lilac turning brown
In the immense silence where I live alone.

It is the transient that touches me, old,
Those light-shot clouds as the sky clears,
A passing glory can still move to tears,
Moments of pure joy like some fairy gold
Too evanescent to be kept or told.
And the cat's soft footfall on the stair
Keeps me alive, makes Nowhere into Here.
At the bottom of the silence it is she
Who speaks of an eternal Now to me.

# Blizzard

Hard to imagine daffodils
Where I see nothing but white veils
Incessant falling of thick snow
In this nowhere, non-landscape
Which has no shadow and no shape,
And holds me fast and holds me deep
And will not cease before I sleep.
Hard to imagine somewhere else
Where life could stir and has a pulse,
And know that somewhere else will be
This very field, changed utterly,
With hosts of daffodils to show
That spring was there under the snow.
New Englanders are skeptical
Of what cannot depend on will,
Yet I should know that this wide range
Of white and green and constant change
Have kept me kindled, on the edge of fear,
Travelling the weather like a mountaineer.

# The Shirley Poppies

## 1

No magician pulling a silk kerchief
Out of a thimble could do as well.
The Shirley poppies cast off hairy caps
And hang, still pleated
Like Fortuny dresses,
Then suddenly open.
Such an explosion,
And so silent!

## 2

Moths might envy the texture
Between paper and silk,
And butterflies applaud
The pristine tissue;
Bees are entranced
By trembling gold, that crown
Of stamens like antennae
Round the hard striped seed.
Was there ever a flower so alive?

## 3

I go out early
To pick all that have opened
Then burn each stem-end with a match
To make it last at least one summer day.
But always the petals plop down
And lie like fallen wings
Before I have had my fill
Of red and frilled pink and white.

It has been a summer of staying poppies . . .
And now their magic is over,
And my obsession.

# After Long Illness

Two geese, four ducks along the shore—
They are the sight I always look for
Crossing the causeway on my way to town.
They are exotic geese, each with a crest,
The ducks, two mallard and two white.
Sometimes the ducks are upside down,
Rumps up, beaks nibbling for fodder,
Sometimes the geese are preening feather.
But always what I hope for most
Is when they swim in a single line
Floating the tide, always together,
Clearly connected in their varied skein—
This is the sight I love the best.

But whatever they do
And wherever they are,
In whatever brilliant or gloomy weather,
They rinse my eyes on my way to town.

What, after all, brings joyful release
After long illness, after near despair,
Better than four ducks and two geese?

So if by chance they are not there
I am cross in the empty-of-joy air,
And feel deprived and suddenly alone
Driving too fast now, cold at the bone.

# Dream

Inside my mother's death
I lay and could not breathe,
Under the hollow cheekbone,
Under the masked face,
As if locked under stone
In that terrible place.

I knew before I woke
That I would have to break
Myself out of that tomb,
Be born again or die,
Once more wrench from the womb
The prisoner's harsh cry.

And that the only way
Was to bring death with me
From under the lost face,
For I would never come
From that empty place
Without her, alone:

Her death within me
Like the roots of a tree,
Her life within mine—
Twice-born mystery
Where the roots intertwine.
When I woke, I was free.

# August Third

These days
Lifting myself up
Like a heavy weight,
Old camel getting to her knees,
I think of my mother
And the inexhaustible flame
That kept her alive
Until she died.

She knew all about fatigue
And how one pushes it aside
For staking up the lilies
Early in the morning,
The way one pushes it aside
For a friend in need,
For a hungry cat.

Mother, be with me.
Today on your birthday
I am older than you were
When you died
Thirty-five years ago.
Thinking of you
The old camel gets to her knees,
Stands up,
Moves forward slowly
Into the new day.

If you taught me one thing
It was never to fail life.

# Salt Lick

They come like deer
To a salt lick,
They come without fear,
Come from far and near
To lick and lick.

The salt, a mystery,
The written word,
Not me.

But the deer, you see,
Are confused.
I, not the word, am used
To fill their need
Like salt or bread.

On some cold winter day
I shall be licked away
Through no deer's fault,
There will be no more salt.

# Two Birthdays

## I

*(for Keith Warren at eighty)*

We come to honor Keith, dear rooted man.
He is our tree, both strong and fragile
For it is eighty years since he began
The long growth upward and the long growth deep,
The spirit springing fresh and ever agile
To balance what is lost and what will keep.

Love keeps, and courage keeps, this man can tell,
Still sweet and spicy and still evergreen
To shelter all of us who know him well
As husband, father, grandfather, and friend.
The tree, well-rooted, strong and serene,
Learned when to stand fast, when slightly to bend.

So taught us when to yield and how to grow,
And how great burdens may be lightly worn.
Through eighty rich years of the shifting snow
This great tree proved its grace under stress.
For courage keeps and love is still newborn,
Greening our whole world with its gentleness.

## II

*(for Edith Morse Johnson at ninety)*

She is as keen as any star
Upon a winter night;
And never weariness, despair,
Bodily ill or childish fear
Can put out undiminished light
Now in its ninetieth year.

If loneliness sometimes at dusk
May wander in her range,
"I put my mind to work, some task,"
She says with passion, "but why ask?
It's intellect can make the change.
I *think* myself out of the past."

The grandchildren of those she taught
Warm hands at the same fire
Of ardor, and concern, and thought
Her students learned when they were caught
Between their fire and her fire
(Learned it upon a classic lyre).

It is great music feeds her mind,
Now she must listen, sharing:
And one might travel far to find
Listener as keen, alive, and kind:
She suffers still the shafts of caring,
And never speaks of going blind.

Call all this easy if you dare—
The joyful pride and bitterness.
I say this life is rare and dear.
We shall not see its like for less
Than what her fiery heart still pays,
So praise, so prize this ninetieth year!

# The House of Gathering

If old age is a house of gathering,
Then the hands are full.
There are old trees to prune
And young plants to plant,
There are seeds to be sown.
Not less of anything
But more of everything
To care for,
To maintain,
To keep sorted out,
A profusion of people
To answer, to respond to.

But we have been ripening
To a greater ease,
Learning to accept
That all hungers cannot be fed,
That saving the world
May be a matter
Of sowing a seed
Not overturning a tyrant,
That we do what we can.

The moment of vision,
The seizure still makes
Its relentless demands:

Work, love, be silent.
Speak.

# Christmas Light

When everyone had gone
I sat in the library
With the small silent tree,
She and I alone.
How softly she shone!

And for the first time then
For the first time this year,
I felt reborn again,
I knew love's presence near.

Love distant, love detached
And strangely without weight,
Was with me in the night
When everyone had gone
And the garland of pure light
Stayed on, stayed on.

# Part II

# Absence

It was always there,
The great white pine,
Shelter and solid comfort.
From the second floor
I could watch red squirrels
Play, nuthatches lead
Their compulsive lives
In its ample branches.

From the third floor
I could turn away
From the glittering ocean
And rest my eyes
On the thick soft green.
In all seasons wind
Murmured through it.
It was always present.
We lived along together.

Until a winter hurricane
Brought it, shuddering,
Down against the house,
Until that quiet strength
Was broken by force.

On the second floor
The windows are empty
And here on the third
Ragged firs
And formless bits of sky
Are only an irritation.
The air is silent.

Must we lose what we love
To know how much we loved it?

It is always there now,
That absence, that awful absence.

# Wilderness Lost

*for Bramble, my cat*

## I

She was the wilderness in me
The secret solitary place
Where grow the healing herbs.
We had recognized each other
Years ago; the bond was deep.

Now since her death
Two seasons ago
The landscape is ghostly.

No small black and gold panther
Steals through the long grasses
And pounces on a mouse.

No one curls up on the terrace wall
Gathering the day together.
No round shadow sits on my sill
Late at night, waiting to be let in,
And then in one jump comes to lie beside me,
A long pillow of purrs along my back.

## II

Distant, passionate one,
I miss you in my bones.
I miss you like my heartbeat.
I have mourned you for nine months.

What does not leave me
Is your great luminous eye
Open to its golden rim,

The darkness so dark, the deepness so deep there
I wanted to go with you to death
But in a few seconds
The needle did its good work.
You had gone—
And in a new time
I grow old without you.

It is all very still now,
The grief washed out.

# The Cosset Lamb

I met the cosset lamb
Carried in human arms
Because, dog-mauled,
Her mother would not nurse her
And baas in desolation
Along the fence.

I met the lamb and was
Stunned by this innocence.
What is there whiter?
Not milk or even bloodroot.
What is there softer?
Not even a fresh snow.
What is there sweeter
Than horizontal ears
And strange blank eyes?
There came a poignant calm,
Then that faint baa
That lingers on . . .
I knew I was
In Paradise.

For all that is so dear
And may be mauled,
For terror and despair
And for help near,
I weep, I am undone.
For all that can be healed,
The cosset lamb you hold,
And what cannot be healed,
The mother in the field,
I pray now I'm alone.

# AIDS

We are stretched to meet a new dimension
Of love, a more demanding range
Where despair and hope must intertwine.
How grow to meet it? Intention
Here can neither move nor change
The raw truth. Death is on the line.
It comes to separate and estrange
Lover from lover in some reckless design.
Where do we go from here?

Fear. Fear. Fear. Fear.

Our world has never been more stark
Or more in peril.
It is very lonely now in the dark.
Lonely and sterile.

And yet in the simple turn of a head
Mercy lives. I heard it when someone said
"I must go now to a dying friend.
Every night at nine I tuck him into bed,
And give him a shot of morphine,"
And added, "I go where I have never been."
I saw he meant into a new discipline
He had not imagined before, and a new grace.

Every day now we meet it face to face.
Every day now devotion is the test.
Through the long hours, the hard, caring nights
We are forging a new union. We are blest.

As closed hands open to each other
Closed lives open to strange tenderness.
We are learning the hard way how to mother.

] 36 [

Who says it is easy? But we have the power.
I watch the faces deepen all around me.
It is the time of change, the saving hour.
The word is not fear, the word we live,
But an old word suddenly made new,
As we learn it again, as we bring it alive:

Love. Love. Love. Love.

# To Those in the Limbo of Illness

You who have been here before,
Waiting,
Not knowing.

Not living,
Not dying.

Waiting

Waiting

While hope, the open wound,
Bleeds
Its life-giving
Life-exhausting
Blood.

In this limbo
Must love
Become an arc?

For the arc,
It has come to me,
Transcends
What it embraces.

# Destinations

Every day we meet these bodies on the road,
The torn-up porcupines like tanks exploded,
The battered cats, dogs, raccoons, dead.
Every road we take is normally bloodied,
Bodies the usual, like thrown-out beer cans,
Or cars abandoned in the fields to rust.
Only these animals were never machines.
It hurts to think of so much living lost,
Of where they wanted to go and never got to,
Of the brute man who killed them for no reason
Simply because he saw no reason not to,
And kills on every day in every season,
And will not look at what he is doing,
To love, himself, or the starving nations,
Slow down and think, consider destinations.
Destructive man, poor rat, just keeps on going.

# New Year Poem

Let us step outside for a moment
As the sun breaks through clouds
And shines on wet newfallen snow,
And breathe the new air.
So much has died that had to die this year.

We are dying away from things.
It is a necessity—we have to do it
Or we shall be buried under the magazines,
The too many clothes, the too much food.
We have dragged it all around
Like dung beetles
Who drag piles of dung
Behind them on which to feed,
In which to lay their eggs.

Let us step outside for a moment
Among ocean, clouds, a white field,
Islands floating in the distance.
They have always been there.
But we have not been there.

We are going to drive slowly
And see the small poor farms,
The lovely shapes of leafless trees
Their shadows blue on the snow.
We are going to learn the sharp edge
Of perception after a day's fast.

There is nothing to fear
About this revolution . . .
Though it will change our minds.

Aggression, violence, machismo
Are fading from us
Like old photographs
Faintly ridiculous
(Did a man actually step like a goose
To instill fear?
Does a boy have to kill
To become a man?)

Already there are signs.
Young people plant gardens.
Fathers change their babies' diapers
And are learning to cook.

Let us step outside for a moment.
It is all there
Only we have been slow to arrive
At a way of seeing it.
Unless the gentle inherit the earth
There will be no earth.

# Part III

*Earlier Poems*

# *How Is It with You, Falcon?*

How is it with you, falcon, in your tower?
Hooded and fierce, serving a hard master,
As often as not you must hoard your power,
Be less than yourself who can move faster
Than any owl after a mousy thought,
As often as not slow your penetration
To keep decorum and to maintain court
(Matters of moment require deliberation).
This subtle control is worn with such lightness,
You show soft wing, not steel pinions,
Not the eye's vision, but its simple brightness.
So you survey your kingdom and dominions.

Here is nothing you have not yourself willed,
The grace to withhold power, the sense of office,
The bright eye hooded, the wild blood stilled—
Wisest of falcons, neither young nor novice,
I have not come with arrogance to ask
What private riches nourish public task.
I note, alive and beautiful, your power:
That is enough for this season and this hour.

# The Question

Soon we shall know whether it was a demon
Throwing a rocklike message at my head,
Or a good angel who brought this fever on,
To stand now, guardian, beside my bed:
I set you here within my solitude
To bear its full weight, for ill or for good.

This house is full of presences (alarmed
By the intrusion of another ghost?).
This house is judge, O shall I have harmed
The hardwon powers that I cherish most?
The demon says, "But poetry is all,"
The angel, "Love must be responsible."

I ponder on the harsh life that you carve,
The uses of your power, and on your soul,
Dear complex being whom I mean to serve.
I know we walk between Heaven and Hell.
The question flares up through the conscious mind,
What in this love, for you, is good or kind?

I want your greatness as I want my own.
And what I sense is the subtle poise
(The time is crucial and as hard as stone)
Just before climax. It is no time for toys.
When were you young enough? Where did heart fail?
Who clothed this woman in a coat of mail?

Even as a collegian your power begins.
You moved within the framework and the laws,
(We poets too start early for our sins),
And yet this stance for power does give me pause.
Did you learn then the sovereign way to chill,
To use charm as a weapon with such skill?

Your college suffers from a loneliness.
These are blunt words: they come from deep concern.
For here you stop just short of your own greatness.
Permit a change, as if spring days could burn
Winter away, and love might play its part,
Simply in the diffusion of a heart.

Take love and use it for what it is worth,
Which is to say, Nourish your starved college:
You failed to notice moonlight on the earth,
But such great shining is a kind of knowledge.
Lacking it, certain powers are starved and starve:
I ponder on the harsh life that you carve.

# The Ghost in the Machine

So you have made your peace with the machine;
It is a masterly ingenious one,
Resolving hard equations and serene,
Through the long days of gifted, clear attention.
Only pure music could give you the lie,
Music, angelic silence—but not I.

After the word "machine," I became still,
Living next day suspended on one thought,
To sharpen spirit back, knit up the will
To meet your courage, so steadfast and so caught.
But only music, Mozartian and stable,
Could make an answer now. I am not able.

Words become heavy in a total dark,
And who is strong enough to bear their weight?
What you gave me was generous, though stark.
That gift I learn—slowly—to contemplate.
But only music at its most clear and noble,
Could answer you with truth. I am not able.

After that word, I lost the power to speak.
I know even machines take loving care.
Complex computers have been known to break:
The ghost in the machine is always there.
But I am silenced, because I am ashamed
That here so little warmed, for all that flamed.

# Song for a Lute

Bright falcon
Prison tower
Source that makes thirsty
River of fire

When I came to the gate with my lute, with my lute,
The guardian said, "Take this kingdom as free;
You may look at the flowers and taste of the fruit,
But never a heavy heart, never a plea,
Or the gate will be forced down over the moat,
And you will be prisoner held for a fee."

Bright falcon
Prison tower
Source that makes thirsty
River of fire

When I came to the tower and saw the young queen,
She smiled a grave smile and I sang to my lute,
But I questioned her face and it was not serene.
I saw the nipped bud. I tasted green fruit,
And heavy my heart for all I had seen,
And joy was a dove that mourned in my throat.

Bright falcon
Prison tower
Source that makes thirsty
River of fire

When I entered that kingdom of arduous joy,
The young queen herself in her sovereign grace
Was a prisoner there and held for a fee;
She smiled a grave smile, but white was her face:

The falcon was hooded, as well as I could see,
And my lute was stilled in that terrible place.

> Bright falcon
> Prison tower
> Source that makes thirsty
> River of fire

So heavy my heart I turned to be gone,
But the gate was forced down over the moat.
If I was a prisoner, so was the queen.
Though I stood at the gate with my lute, with my lute,
I knew the bright falcon would never be flown,
And for her duress, the joy died in my throat.

# A Cold Day

"Madame, il fait grand froid, et j'ai tué six loups":
My father loved this imaginary letter
And quoted it, smiling at dear old Victor Hugo
Who invented and thus addressed an imaginary queen.
Succinct and noble—could one do it better?
Ma'am, no romantic poet ever invented you.
Entranced, I watch you playing your own scene.

It is a tame world today in your Academy,
Strange world filled with the self-tormenting young,
And the middle-aged in their awful self-possession.
What a poet is doing here will always puzzle me,
The haunted hunter who treads soft after a song,
But whatever she learns, will never learn discretion.
Madame, the day is cold. The hunt has gone wrong.

I will lay down this sudden madness when I move
Into the presence of my students, the unarmed,
The vulnerable, the passionate, whom I regard
With such a different kind of detached love.
The cold affects them also; they are not to be harmed
Whose whole lives hang on the honest spoken word.
It is a cold day, Ma'am: they will be warmed.

And not for long will this empty hunt halloo its way
Through the tame groves after untameable truth;
Long long ago, I am told, the wolves were lean,
But those lithe shadows have recently stolen away,
And poets sneer who uttered fire in their youth.
Ma'am, it is too cold here even for spleen:
I beg you to warm yourself at the fire of myth.

Would you call feeling off, that wolf, that stranger
Who lopes with golden eyes the sacred wood,

A touch of wildness . . . is it too great a risk?
I am your servant and will track down danger,
But you are not Little Red Riding Hood,
And may not poets smile and dare to ask,
*Madame, faut-il tuer le dernier loup?*

# Moment of Truth

The moment of truth, when the bull dies—
Just here in this penitential room,
Or bare arena before unclouded eyes,
And the sad bull begins to long for home.

He has suffered from, fought with too much light,
The arid sands and the public noise,
And bends his head toward darkness and night,
Toward an end to bitter public joys.

Is he the mystical beast whom crowds applaud
Because he bears their violence to death?
Brave brute whom even queens may sometimes laud,
Throwing a rose down to the staggered breath?

If we must do him in, poor passion,
The mythical beast, too rough and bold,
Then give him the moment of truth in royal fashion:
Show me your warmth, Ma'am. You and I grow old.

Show me your warmth unshielded, tell me true
In this arena where the myths grow dumb
That worlds may perhaps be shaken, but not you.
Take this bull by the horns inside the dream.

Or—let me put off the papier-mâché head
Painfully wrought to turn truth to a game,
And let the myth sleep in its timeless bed,
And let me call you by your human name.

I cannot say it without some memory
Of desolation threading through the light:
I turn, gentled, toward your delicate beauty,
But feel the darkness rising in my throat.

# OVER TROUBLED WATER

I sit at my desk in a huge silence
Alone after the loud traffic in the will.
Buffeted by those troubling deep currents
That would not let me land or soul be still.
Dear God, help me to close my open eyes.
Help me to lift up from the inmost place
A silence huge as that above wild skies,
As secret as your always absent Face.
Give me your darkness, your austere demand.
Strip me of every brilliant autumn leaf,
And lay the weight of reason in my hand.
Give me your darkness beyond hope or grief
Where the heartbeat itself cannot be heard,
God of creation, Oh huge silent Word!

Literal now, the trembling and the fear,
Ache in the bones and piercing of the heart.
Between us nothing now is safe or clear,
And apprehension like an ugly wart
Has managed to affect even the soul.
I walk a fine edge, careful for your peace,
Deep in my center hold the center still,
And would atone, or give you some release,
But what I am comes from a range of seeing
Outside your range and dangerous for you.
I cannot offer less than my whole being;
Your doubts and fears come from the whole of you.
We deal in essence, but deep in the mind
Love is a high explosive—and not kind.

The poet dances on a rope held taut
Between reality and his desire;
The acrobat of feeling trained by thought,
He disciplines himself upon the wire
And in achieving perfect balance
Is burned, is rocked, and suffers for the cool
He did not learn through any lucky chance.
That grace was taught him in a cruel school:
Either you sublimate, my friend, or fall
Into confused, confusing human hell
Where even ardor becomes pitiful—
"A poor performer, he did not do it well."
The poet lives on peril and to give
Joy from his pain, a curious kind of love.

Love cannot act, and so I must embark,
Fragile, a paper boat upon a stream,
Into the deep recesses of my dark,
Into the isolation of the dream
Where archetypal figures may still roam,
Where shines the innocence of unicorn,
And where the flaming phoenix builds his home,
And Poetry, the sacred beast forlorn,
Stumbles forever uncaressed, alone,
The child of passion married to despair,
As if, poor beast, it were his to atone
For love that cannot act, that is nowhere,
That never will find rest, that cannot sleep,
Mystical creature, wandering the deep.

We know the legend of clear loving eyes
That see through the encasement of some beast,
Sad frog or donkey, a prince in disguise,
Who wait an act of grace to be released.
The legend asks a lady without fear
To lay her hand in a smiling caress
On poor wart-face, or stroke a fur-lined ear,
And bring about the metamorphosis—
A princess like a gentle lunatic
Who wanders, dreaming, into a sacred place,
One who feels love and does not question it,
But gently blesses monster's antic face,
Risks her identity for his disguise
Because she has looked deep into his eyes.

The legend haunts us still. Each of us wears
Disguise or mask, longs to be taken in—
From deep inside the beast, prince stares,
The myth of childhood intact, evergreen.
I startled you by putting it so plain:
Poetry like the beast lives in disguise
And waits a sovereign touch to end its pain.
Lately I cannot look you in the eyes,
For poetry, once prince, legend reversed,
Turns into beast for lack of your touch.
Arid my art, unfertilized and cursed.
You stay behind your mask beyond its reach.
Legend reversed, this true love without trust
Turns prince to beast and poetry to lust.

If you take refuge in a word then bear
The word you use against me, "puritan."
A name for those most fearful when they care,
Those who give little and love lean
Rather than risk the soul to shallow pleasure.
How do you think I live? The suspect image
Of all you most dread and must treasure,
The anti-puritan, a childlike mage?
I live with miracles, touch of your hand,
The lightest petal, snowfall on my skin,
All take me to the overwhelming land
Where feeling can be blest and is no sin.
No shallow pleasure here, but the grave joys
That spring from poetry and give it poise.

Last night I stood beside you in your hell,
That desert seared to nothing but dry sand,
Where only ghosts are welcome or feel well,
And memory itself can fill your hand
Only with dust for icy winds to blow.
No root finds water in this cruel place,
No wing finds shelter, nothing may grow.
No human tears are seen on any face;
The hollow eyes stare out masked and unseeing,
As if from a bronze head buried in waste,
The prisoner inside long dead to being,
No ears to hear, no mouth to speak or taste.
I weep no tears. I live in your despair.
You are my hell and you will meet me there.

It's the time of breaking, your house sold,
Our time together shattered like a mirror
Where partial love, too fearful or too bold,
Never quite made it into peace or fervor.
Each met himself but failed to meet the other
In that locked surface. Time to take
The image of the dreadful wooden mother
And break it now with all we have to break,
The image of a dirtied copybook,
A lover half accepted, half denied,
The guilt you suffered for a loving look,
The guilt I suffered when I raged and cried,
Who kissed your hands, who slept in your bed
To meet your empty eyes, closed marble head.

So there was, after all, no destination
For this long passionate journey in the head,
The journey into exile, desolation
After the sleepless nights, rumor and dread,
The sudden breakdowns when our nerves were jangled,
While a romantic landscape came and went,
So triste and boring it was good we wrangled,
Passengers forced to cross the land of Want,
Carried by fits and starts toward Nowhere.
The future lost its image to the past.
We lived in that stale over-heated air,
And under skies too often overcast,
Exiles within a train called Desolation
That never stops because there is no station.

We got off where we started months ago.
There was no one to meet us, no hot tea
In the deserted village lost in snow,
Where nothing but a servant's jealousy
Could animate or rouse a moment's rage
And bring the flush of passion to your cheek.
And so we part on this provincial stage,
The play too long, the actors ill or weak,
Exhausted by the long tour through frustration.
It had its moments but they did not last
Since your despair must follow on elation
And all my true words died for lack of trust.
Now in a house dismantled, the stage set,
Two ghostly lovers part who never met.

# The Muse as Donkey

## I

Deprived of the true source,
I have borrowed a donkey for the summer.
Her name is Desperation,
Or perhaps Wild Hope.

When I turn in my chair
I see her in the meadow,
Gray presence among daisies,
Long ears pointed forward,
Her tail rising and falling
Like a pendulum.

Sometimes she utters
A silent bray.
I understand.
I am desperate myself
In the middle of this damp, green,
Intolerable June.

## II

I am a practical person,
Pull weeds, make lists,
Answer letters,
Talk to the donkey.
Stroke her nose, soft as velvet.
My sneakered feet are never dry
This wet summer.
Do you believe me?

I am a practical person.
You can tell that, surely.

It is enough that the poppy
Bursts the hard shell of its bud,
And opens,
Though it looked impossible.
I live with reality here.

Yet for five long years
The White Goddess
Commanded my being.
I was borne on great tides,
Waves stormed in my head.
I was washed up
On terrible shores
Alone.

For five years
I lived with signs and omens.
I was sent on adventures.
The lists became poems.

Do you believe me?
There are mysteries,
Sources, an underground river
On the other side of the mountain
Of self-doubt,
And of rejection,
As real as the donkey's nose,
As real as the huge red poppy
Open.

Do you believe me?
It would help if you did,
Help me
Not to die the death
Of the rejected
Who deny their vision.

] 66 [

# III

I shall tell you the signs,
The omens,
Owls, moons.

I was on a highway
Which might have taken me
To the white Goddess,
But at the turn-off
Within an island of trees
A Great White Owl
Sat on a pine bough,
Tremendous.
It was full daylight.
I took it as an omen.
I did not risk the encounter.

Before that,
When I was on my way to see her,
From a distance,
In a public place,
A dead owl lay on the road,
Still warm.
I could lift the great soft wing
To its full span,
Brown and white.
I saw strong yellow legs
And a terrible beak.

Tenderly I carried my broken friend
To a shelter of grass.
Tears broke out of me
Like tears out of rock.
I knew there was hard news
Ahead.

The full moon
Has often attended
A moment of grace,
But the last time
I came with my question,
And dialled her number,
The answer was "no".
And I learned
As I sat in the strangest darkness
That the moon at that second
Went into eclipse.

These are crude
Signs, crude omens.
But I can tell you
That I have grown a third ear
Listening,
Keeping the silence alive.
My clouded eyes have seen
The head of Medusa
Calm in sleep.
Not all dreams are lies.

## IV

Ilumination costs.
There is also the violence.
How does the poppy burst out
From that coarse harsh bud
Except by force?

The White Goddess
Is a hard one to serve.
Asks patience.
No questions.
No private wishes.
The serene no-will.
She demands poems.

Ask for a glimpse of her face again
And you will be beaten down.

I had waited five years
For the resolution,
To know once and for all
What was dream, what reality.

I asked.
I was beaten down.

The tension went slack.
The tightrope lay on the ground
And the tightrope walker's feet
Faltered.
There was nowhere to go.

I am a practical person.
I ate dirt.
I ground my teeth on pebbles.
I am a practical person.
I borrowed a donkey.

When I saw the long ears
In the truck,
It was kingdom come.

It was patience
Come to this gentle place
Where only I am violent,
Unregenerate,
Full of rage and anguish,
Never at peace,
Among the silent flowers,
The cool calming trees,
This tranquil order.
This house. This garden.

I created it
Like a mad woman
Who bends over an intricate,
Never-to-be-finished
Piece of sewing
To keep her from screaming.

For the White goddess—
She who will never come—
I created it,
Tangible sign
Of an invisible world.

Now when I look up
The donkey stands in the meadow,
Flapping her long ears
As if she had come to stay.
Unable to heal myself,
I shall spend the summer
Healing the donkey . . .
Already she runs
On her arthritic ankles.
She has learned to bray aloud.

I am a practical person.
Let us believe
That Mystery itself is fulfillment.
It was given to me
To be deeply stirred
To be taken out of myself
By the "evidence of things not seen."
Now the donkey's frail ankles
Absorb my heart,
We are fellow-sufferers,
And we do not despair.

# Part IV

# Invocation

Never has the sea been maternal to me or kind
But always cruel master of separations,
Where the mind wanders and the heart goes blind
Dreaming and empty under the slow swaying.
Never, never shall I call the sea mother.
It is the place of awful childhood fear,
Death by water, death by separation,
When what I do not want to lose is lost
To me, gone beyond my will at landfall
(Many times a person, once it was a country).

But I shall be with you this long voyage,
Your image at the prow, exultant as a dolphin.

And when the gulls hang on our wind at landfall
Be with me, Goddess, rising out of the wave
Wrapped in bright air, your hands tasting of salt,
Your hair gold as the delicate branch of myrtle
Laid on the Grecian grave-jar, immortal love.
Aphrodite, be with me at this strange landing!

# The Skilled Man

*for Bill Vaughan*

If someone should ask me how
A poem is whittled and willed,
Just how it is done, you know,
With what love both wary and skilled,
I'd suggest that he watch Bill make
A thing that does not look hard
Like this staff for an old knife,
And learn that all that it takes
To make a knife new or a word
Is the subtle exchange of a life.

# The Smile

*Stefano Sassetta*

Angels are grave if they exist at all
Lifted above the gritty frustration
The lonely spendthrift way we live.
They wing it upwards where we stumble,
Space, air and light their habitation,
Distance their message beyond love.

But here the painter dreamed a different kind,
An angel of the earth secretly smiling.
She listens with a plain astonished face
Full of delight at what her fingers find
To music which she hears as so beguiling,
Herself, her lute become amazing grace.

And I am suddenly transported here
Into the always saving joy and thrust
Of pure creation, seized by the hair,
The shock of this angel's atmosphere,
And thrown up to the sky in a wild gust
That blows to pieces anger and despair.

# The Phoenix Again

On the ashes of this nest
Love wove with deathly fire
The phoenix takes its rest
Forgetting all desire.

After the flame, a pause,
After the pain, rebirth.
Obeying nature's laws
The phoenix goes to earth.

You cannot call it old
You cannot call it young.
No phoenix can be told,
This is the end of song.

It struggles now alone
Against death and self-doubt,
But underneath the bone
The wings are pushing out.

And one cold starry night
Whatever your belief
The phoenix will take flight
Over the seas of grief

To sing her thrilling song
To stars and waves and sky
For neither old nor young
The phoenix does not die.

# Index of Titles and First Lines